emerge

FRANCESCA MARAIS

Francesca Marais was born and raised in South Africa and now lives in NYC. She went to university in Arizona for a degree in information systems, but has been writing poetry since she was thirteen years old, as a form of journaling and self-expression. Francesca continues to explore the world in parts, through pen and paper.

—

—

Francesca Marais
theblackrose.journal@gmail.com

—

ISBN 978-0-578-75937-1
Printed in the United States of America.
First Printing, 2020.

Dedication

To my mother, who's seen my dreams bigger than I've been able to, thank you. To the friends who've read or listened, encouraged my work, and watched me at an open mic—I share the joy in seeing this come to life with you! To people who've touched my soul and sparked inspiration in me, one way or another, thank you.

Contents

Acknowledgments

My first chapbook editor's guidance and expertise pushed me deeper into my work and encouraged me to skim off excess and rearrange it into a creative piece. Thank you, Kallie.

Bookworm

We are not whimsical.
We only cherished our calling
And learned that through it
We could safely escape
Rattling instability,
Where our safety and fears
Were in our own hands.

We are not whimsical
When only the thought of hearing our mother's voice near
Was our strength to push
Us through
One page after another
Living to pursue the next day's tale,
So that our journey could be recounted
In our own words, through our own actions
And our own voices.

We are not whimsical
When we choose to listen to those who speak
To learn our true ways in our silence
Where our voice teaches a yearning
And gives a name to our uncompromising needs
Free from malice and overheard judgment.
Our silence was learned through fear.
Our silence taught us strength,
Where dreams had vision
And seemed within grasp.

It is within that we sought recourse.

It is through withdrawing from the incessant reel
that we learned to love.

We aspire beyond our measure
To tread a future we eagerly desire,
To savour defeating the antagonist,
To welcome happiness and redefine
Selfless love,
To rewrite our story in the ways
We always read.

We are not whimsical.

Fairy Tale

There are many stories I've
Come to learn in my upbringing—
That of the Zim-Zim, a monster
That traverses townships in the night
Looking for idle minds to devour.

I've heard of the Tokoloshe,
Ancient in his time,
But feared by all tribes in the nation.
Witchcraft, sorcery,
Name it what you will.

My head slightly
Peeking from the covers
As my grandmother told each
Of these tales,
A different bedtime story
That kept me in my graces.

Each of these monsters
Possessed the power to evoke Terror
in their prey.
I always prayed that I would
Never see them.
I prayed for all the good in the world.

I prayed to never be in trouble

Or caught making it.
I prayed every night,
Holy worship, with the Holy Ghost
Always present in my
Grandmother's church

In the copper and silver staff.
I believed in God
Or a power beyond
My preteen grasp.
I always knew these prayers had some clout,
Felt they must work
For how hard we prayed.

I prayed throughout my life,
Gave alms to the Church,
Became a catechist,
And felt my duty in deed
Was being done.

I heard many stories, through
The Church,
Through family, of other members
Whom I saw come and go.

There was one story I lived
Through—
A childlike fairy tale

Of a young princess
Whose kingly father
Came to take part in the script
And end scene with good heart.

That tale had multiple scenes
Relived through faint memory
Yet invoking sentiment
As vivid as a lucid dream.

End scene, the story cut,
It fast-forwards to the future.
Ahead of me, the curtain call.
Heads bowing down before me,
I could only see the crown.

Inheritance

As the wind blows,
Man's heart sways in time
To the beat of his reverberating pulse.
In his eyes, the centuries of promise
Overpower his memory of what he wanted and lost,
A fight to see his legacy fortified,
His final gift.
Through his children's eyes,
He sees his lessons in their upbringing.
He sees them bloom amidst their agony—
Their ability to prevail, his joy.
In the smiles of his children,
He sees the youth he once knew
And how it continues in them—
Their tears,
The long embraces they seek to bury their loss in.
He feels a heaviness like a cross carried on his back—
The burdens of life finally bearing fruit.
Through the camaraderie in neighbourly conversations,
His children, and their stories,
He lived.

Grief

I learned that grief is a way
Families truly unite.
In their suffering they share
A bond they gradually
Lost touch with.
In their tears and shared condolences,
They remembered who they were.

In life and nearness to death,
We encounter thin places
And our attachment to our
Houses of earthly delights
No longer carry the weight of
Their wealth.

The silence
Speaks louder than
The heaving sobs.
The silence
Cradles each one
In humility.

In grief, we learn to extend our
Hands and arms in comfort.
In grief, we let down our guards
And our façades crumble, becoming vulnerable
In ourselves.
Our bonds strengthen in warm embrace,
Our tears providing

Consolation in acknowledging the pain in our
Cousins', uncles', and aunts' eyes.

If only the victory of escaping
This town where we bury our beloved
Would mirror this kinship,
Then we wouldn't have needed
To say goodbye.

Insomnia

And there are days when
I wake up and never seem to be
Awake.
Mind and body lay in bed
As if there were neither me nor you,
Nor night nor day.
I still
Lay
In day
Or night.
Mind's reason to believe
In a reason beyond dreaming.
Still
Unconsciously,
Waking mind and soul
Borne in the depth of a slumber
Weakened by the idea of soles
Moving step-by-step
On neither air nor ground.
Still
Lay.

Eu Fujo (Escape)

Taking refuge in the abyssal zone of the ocean,

No one else knows
The depths of the unostentatiously receding currents,
Pulling me in from that sunny postcard-beach.

Immersed in a tangle of wrought tentacles,
Wrapping around my chest and anchoring me,

Dependence on
The emptiness of an unknown tomorrow,

Unforgiven hidden romance or its fantasy to be forgotten,
Running headfirst into the waves of my illicit lover's comforting
embrace;
They crash into the day's break.

Believers doubt,
Discredit the what-is-yet-to-come.

My now
Undefined,
Unfulfilled with the wealth of a heart full,

Filled with a yearning to be released from the anchor, into my
lover's arms,
To become what is outside,

To make the within,

I am unfound.

Mother's Ruin

I come here to leave,
Not to escape.
To become the aftermath of the after-hours crowd.
We are in unison in this,
Here now,
Divided only by burnout this city
Now brings us,

Me and you, here.

Oxygenated by the liquid pours,
My soul to my new neighbour
Cannot help but pore
Into your eye's depths,

Seeking the story the lips will not dare tell.

Round on the house
Or on me,
Blurry at this point.

Unfolding nothing, countless pours
Leading into bottomless pits,
Starry nights sparkle in those
Candlelit eyes.

Forget me not,

Though by morning memory of
Lest we forget where we came from.

Where we always return.

Jaded

A cloud in the sky,
I can see the gray in your eyes,
The shafts of light through the shades—
Undeniable.
It was easy to surmise
The power of gaze and silence,
The brush against your lips,
Your hands interlocking mine—
Asking everything with nothing,
Giving everything without wanting.

A Day in Denmark

Slight goosebumps
Begin to form
At the sight of your form—
On the back of my neck,
On my arms, padded by the warmth
Of my goose-feathered winter coat,
Through the sleeves of my woolen shirt.

A slight tremble shaking me to the marrow,
Blood thumping through my veins,
Rushing,
Reverberations echoing through my flesh.
But outside

There is no sound.
The crowds move.

The shape of the form
Becomes the glimmer of stern but endearing
Glass-blue eyes brought into near sight
Only surrounding noise

Cannot surrender.

Shifting
Into your presence
Blood surges through my body,
Refusing to gently creep into the shores
Of my heart's quiet: peace.

Your words
Swim deep into the oceans of my mind
Beyond my grasp,
Filling the space.
Outside myself the noise surfaces.

Faces reappear: it's been a few moments.
I'm calm, it is calm, calm.

I hear and I see you.
I feel you though your touch
Is at arm's distance:
Apart
So far
But beside you
Sitting near.

I feel the torrent in the chords of your voice.
I feel as you look toward me
And I refrain from looking back,
Afraid to see what I want
And then also what I cannot.

I am slightly lifted
And falling heavily into your heart's ebb and flow,
The words you say with your eyes.
We speak,
The easy drift into verbose nothing.
We hear,

Moving me with silence,
Embracing me with all,
Without the soft touch of your fingertips.

Your voice drowns in polite exchange and disdainful inspection;
I submerge into your arms.

Journey

The only time I will submit to you
Is when I am under you.
The only time you will get me to be the person you want to be
Is when I want you.

Life contorts itself into a map of crossroads
I bear to overtake to see myself in a pin-drop.

Driving nowhere in the exitless roundabout
Less you when I am me
In my journeys of this wonderful earth.

I see you but I do not breathe you.
I hear you but I do not care to bear you
Like my mother bore me into my being.

The Christ in life I have sought to see
Has led me forty days and nights
Alone into the desert, beside you.
When I am around you,

Life foreshadows the shadows borne,
Birthed into stories retold.
Mother speaks the words of her youth
She sees in you.

Yet in her words
The wisdom we have known not to understand yet,
The free in freedom we torture ourselves to find,

Seeking immeasurably for pleasures to the mind unforetold.
In the sea
I saw across many shores.

It was still your face that I saw,
The reflection of the you
You once knew,

My horizons were set
En route but diverged into you.

A Man

I am afraid of you
And of all the things you say.

I sit
Here
And stare
Hoping
To gauge your thoughts.

But I am

Amiss.

All

Is despair.

I speak,
Mouthing thoughts I think
You want me to say,
Things
You might
Want to hear,
Hoping
To catch the skip in your heartbeat.
I burrow into the empty earth of your brows,

Force a reading
Of a future so far gone
No stargazer
Or fortune-teller could paint so clear.
So clear,
Almost invisible,
Or just not here.

"O patria mia"
Your arms appear to be
The red-hot mantle fueling my being,

My soles moving me constantly
In your direction,
Senseless in
Closeness,
Almost a

Resuscitation or
Dazzling across the dark night
In the thicket of your
Mind's unknown.

Yet still
Into the vacant, silent gaze,
I seek to find me
In you
And feel what I need to feel
To be.

ALS

The brush of your fingernails against
The back of my neck.
The wisps of your breath against my skin.
The wet trickle of tears down my face.
The salty tear falling between the quiver of my lips
As I try to tell you I love you,
As I try and tremble in anger and frustration,
But cannot utter a word to express.
Piercing eyes and a strained,
Unintentional smile is all.
To hug and to hold you has brought my soul to its knees.
Now that I can no longer,
I am no longer me.
I feel now more than ever
And have so much more to show.
But my body
Atrophied,
Diluting my primal
Presence that once
Garnered look-back stares.

Free

My heart is filled with the empty.
In your fear and need to be fearless,
I sense the part of you—
The ardour—
To be
Liberated in movement,
In speech,
Your chaotic, free tranquility.
In my hand you seek

I want to be the everything.
In my boundaries,
I see no in-between—
The bonds unspoken,
The pent-up carbon
In a shaken Coca Cola bottle readying
To be released.

I tell you,
Let go.

Be with your true self.
Seek within the belly
Your truth.
Depart from the attic you keep going back to.
Cherish then savour
The salt of the pain,
Lick your fingers dry.

I tell you,
Let go.

Conceited

It's so weird how when you laugh,
The top of your nose cringes.
Your eyes, a bountiful brown,
They begin to squint almost shut

And the tears begin.

They tumble down as if over rolling hills,
While your chest and shoulders
Heave with the glee.

It's so weird how your defined cheeks
Begin to "rose"
With the laughter,
Simultaneously seem to
Help your eyes close
Tighter

As if recollecting the best part
Of your trip to a distant land.

It's these and more
That I've grown to love,
That I've seen in your
Own discomfort,
You rise above
Still
Arms wide open.

It's this wide, toothy smile,
Contagious laugh
That your body follows.
Those smiling eyes
Gleaming with joy.

It's you I've come to know
In all your weird, beautiful rebellion.
It is you
That I've grown to love.

Desideratum

Is the need for a male figure
A reason for treason,
My sistah?

Is the need to seek the image you've seen
Time and again

Chasing freshly blown bubbles on a spring day,
Following, waiting to see
As each one pops?

To fill what need, may you please
Give more more more
Than you can possibly have
And take the little you receive only
To beg for mercy?

Led by a lingering scent
I caught a whiff of,
Dying love requited,
Varnished with coats of perfume,
Sweaty sex you cover me up,
Smell my wealth,
Empty these thoughts,
Drown the conscious being
Inside me,
Make me forget my needs,
My seeking to find
The left part of what I think is right,
Always seeming to be right in front of me.

Show me mercy.

Finding the path back to
Selfless love in pain,
Boundaries beyond your white picket fence.
Giving back what I never asked to give.

Show me mercy.

Salivating at the fallacy
Of your phallic strength and prowess—
It's all for show.

Show me mercy. Show me truth.

www.ingramcontent.com/pod-product-compliance
Lightning Source LLC
Chambersburg PA
CBHW040941100426
42813CB00017B/2889